MISTER ROGERS TALKS ABOUT

THE NEW BABY
MOVING
FIGHTING
GOING TO THE DOCTOR
GOING TO SCHOOL
HAIRCUTS

by Fred Rogers

Photographs by Myron Papiz

Platt & Munk, Publishers/New York

Acknowledgements:

Some of the photos reproduced in this book were taken courtesy of the Children's Health Center and Hospital; Community University Health Care Center; Institute of Child Development, University of Minnesota; Dr. Michael J. Kozak; Metcalf-Mayflower Moving and Storage Co.; Northrop Collegiate School; Pratt-Motley Continuous Progress Elementary School; Dr. Barbara Schulte; Dr. Charles Hilton Schulte, and Dr. Omar A. Tveten — all of Minneapolis.

TABLE OF CONTENTS

A Message to Parents

Children have amazing resources for coping with life when they and their adults are in warm communication with each other.

A father said to me, "I am often at a loss for the right words to talk with my little boy. I don't want to talk down to him, but I don't want to use words that are too hard for him either. Since I've watched Mister Rogers talking to children on television, I've gotten some ideas of my own about how to answer my boy's questions, and how to tell him about things that I know are important to him even when he doesn't ask."

MISTER ROGERS TALKS ABOUT is a book for parents and children to enjoy together. Each chapter is about experiences children often have, like getting a haircut or going to the doctor. Some are about family experiences that children share with adults, such as the coming of a new baby, or moving from a familiar home to one that is at first unfamiliar. Mister Rogers offers these discussions not as a substitute for parents and children talking with each other about these important events, but rather as a way of introducing subjects that parents and children will be discussing together. Although there are common experiences and worries that all children share, each child and his family have special things that are unique to them. Mister Rogers' book is offered to families as a support in open communication between children and parents about things that are important to them as they develop.

Margaret McFarland, Ph.D.

THE NEW BABY

When a new baby comes to your house . . .

It's really a nice baby,
but everybody spends so much time
looking at it,
and holding it,
and making faces at it.

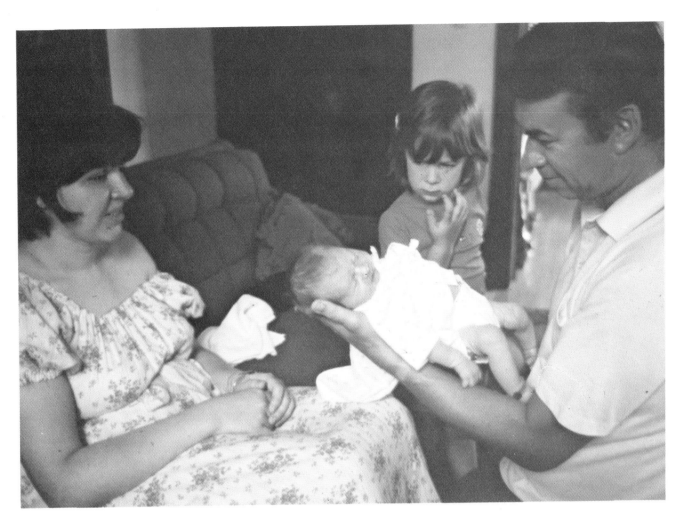

They seem to have less time for you.

The baby sleeps in a crib. You once
slept in a bed like that when *you* were
a baby.

Did the new baby get your old crib?
Did the new baby get some of your old things?
You have something special that the new
baby doesn't have.
You are the older one and you have a
special place in the family.

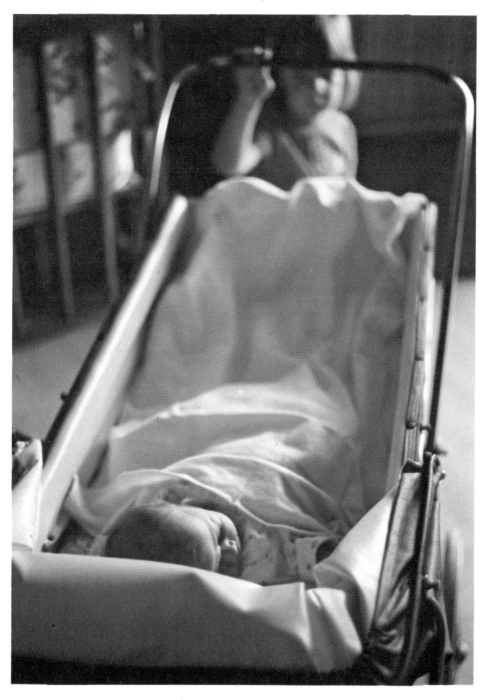

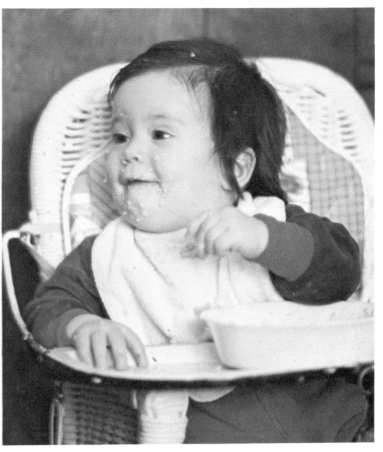

When the baby sits and stares some people try to make it laugh.

When the baby makes a mess at dinner some people think that's cute.

When the baby takes out all the pots and pans, hardly anyone yells and says to put them all back.

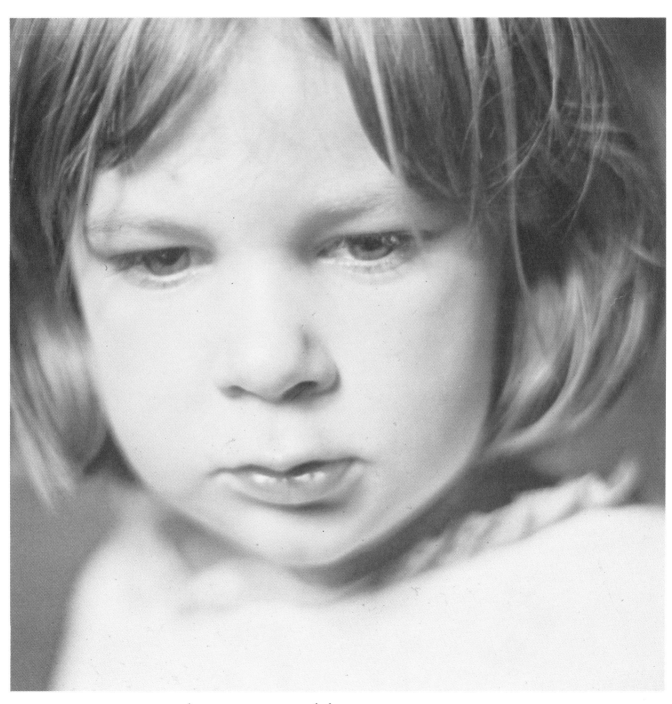

A person could get very grumpy.

But the new baby is too little to know
how to do very many things.

The new baby has lots of things to learn,
and you can help.

When the baby is bigger, you can
show the baby how to crawl
or how to walk.

Because you're the older one you can show the baby lots of things.

Bike riding

Swinging

Climbing

You can even help the baby understand about pretending.

The new baby needs you for sad and lonely
times, too. That's another thing brothers and sisters
are very good for.

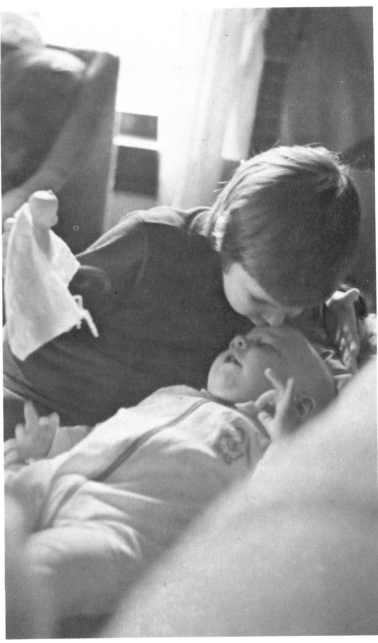

And that's what families are good for, too . . .

caring about each other . . . in all kinds of ways.

When a baby comes to your house
you're the older one. You have your
own place in the family and that place
will always be yours.

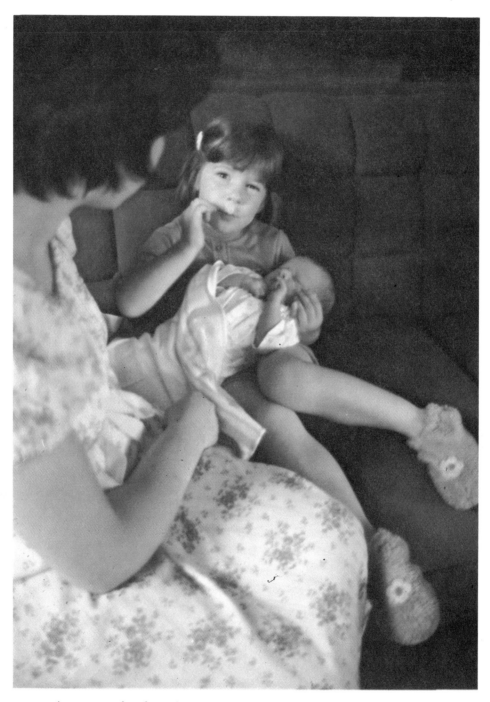

A new baby is one more person to love
and care about you.

• • •

MOVING

People don't always live in the same place forever.

When parents decide to move from one home
to another, their children go with them.

Sometimes people
practice moving.

They pack their
suitcases.

They stay overnight with a friend.

They even pretend that they're living in a new home already.

But when people really move, they're usually sad because they're going away from people that they care about. They're leaving their neighbors or their playmates.

Even though they are usually sad on the day that they move, sometimes they can go back and visit, or call those people on the telephone, or even send cards in the mail.

And people are often
irritable on moving days, too.

There's so much to do and
everything seems to be
out of place.

But people still love and care
about other people,
even when they're irritable.

People usually have so many things to take with them when they move that they need a truck to carry it all.

When they get to their new home, all those things
that they put on the truck will come out of the
truck again and go into their new place.

It may seem funny to have those things in a
different house — beds, pots and pans, tools,
curtains and books, all those things — but
pretty soon that new house will seem like
home again.

In the new place they'll even find new neighbors, new friends. Of course, they'll be different from their neighbors and friends in the old neighborhood, but they can get to like some of the new ones very much, too.

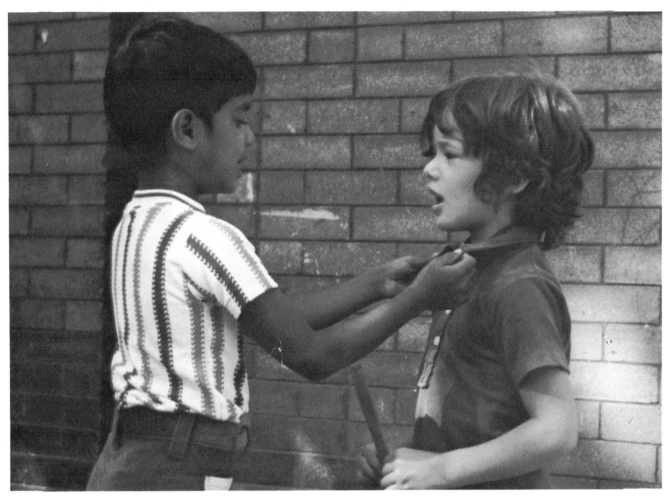

Did you ever know anybody who moved to a new home?
If there are people who have just moved to your
neighborhood, they could tell you lots of things about
moving: what they did and how they felt. Since
you're their new neighbor, you might be their
new friend.

• • •

FIGHTING

There are some times when people fight.

When you play by yourself,
you do things your own way.

Nobody is exactly alike,
so nobody does things
exactly the same way.

Sometimes you like to do
things with other people.

Things together.
When you do things together, you
have to decide together how to
do them.

But when you want to do things exactly
your way, and other people want to do
things exactly their way . . .
sometimes you get angry.

Sometimes you both want to play with the same toy at the same time. But you don't want to play with it together.

Sometimes you don't want to wait your turn.

Sometimes
you both want
to be in the same
place at the
same time.

When your friend says something
that makes you feel angry,
sometimes you shout.

And sometimes you cry.

Sometimes you even feel so bad
you wish the world would go away.

But when you feel sad
or angry you know
you can tell somebody
who is older.

Older people can help
younger people feel
a lot better.

It isn't easy to talk about it when you're angry.

But sometimes it works.

You can even tell the person
who made you angry how you feel.

Real friends make it work.

• • •

GOING TO THE DOCTOR

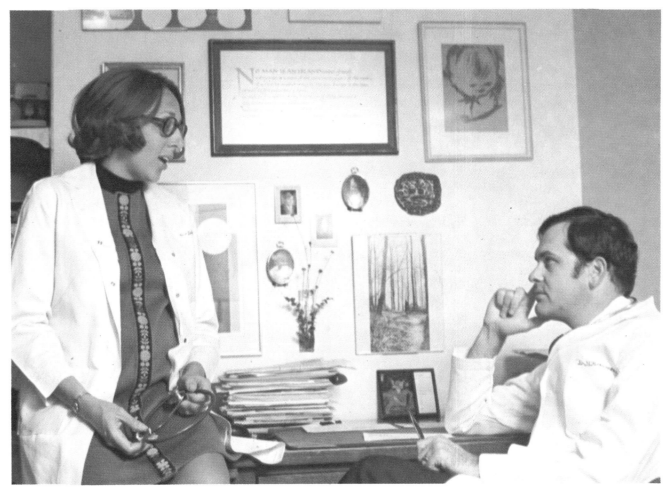

Women can be doctors
and
Men can be doctors.

Doctors were children once who grew up and wanted to take care of people in a special way. They had to study and learn about people's bodies and their feelings.

It's only after all that learning and lots of practice that a doctor is ready to take care of you. Doctors are meant to take good care of people.

The doctor takes care of many people each day,
so sometimes you have to wait your turn in
a special room called the WAITING ROOM.

Waiting can be hard sometimes, but you can
think of things to do while you're waiting.

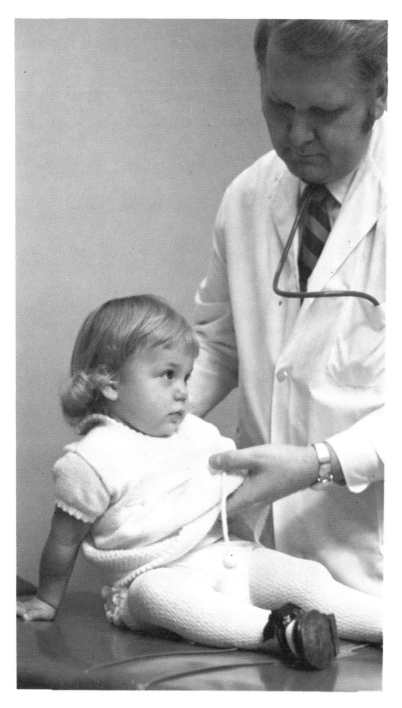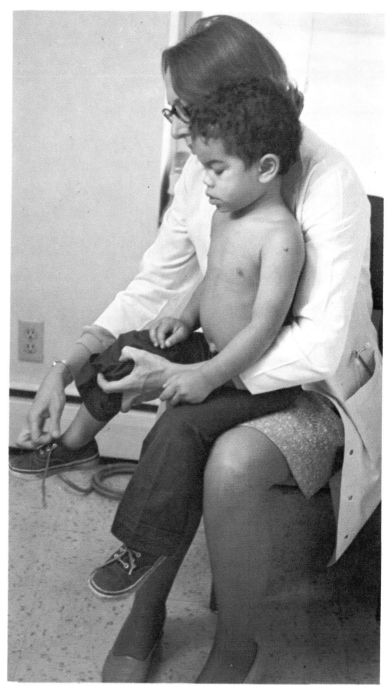

In the doctor's office people often need to undress so the doctor can make sure their bodies are healthy all over. That's what doctors are interested in — getting you better when you're sick and keeping you healthy so you can grow.

The doctor often measures you and weighs you on the scale to see how much you've grown since you were there last time.

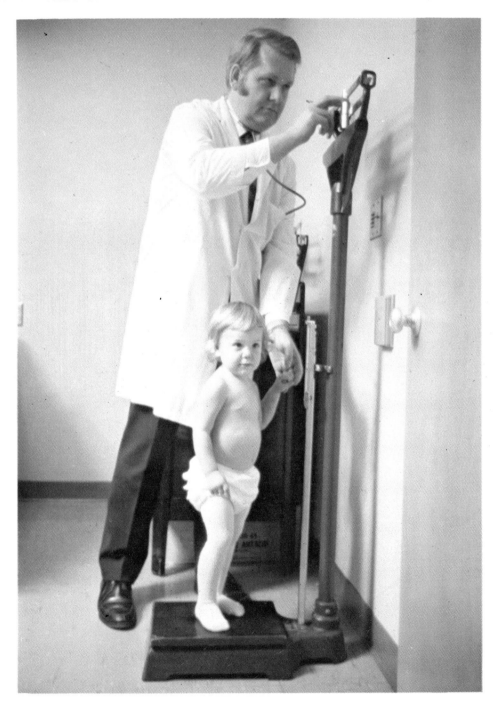

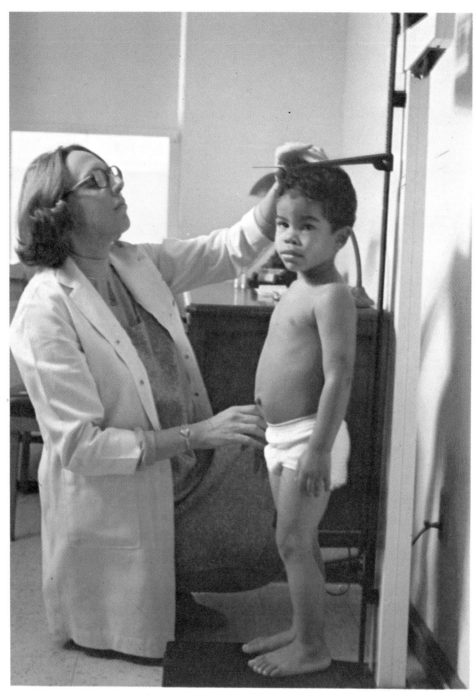

The doctor wants to see how tall you are *without* your shoes.

Inside the examining room the doctor looks
in your mouth. The doctor sometimes
presses down your tongue for a moment so
it's easy to see your throat.

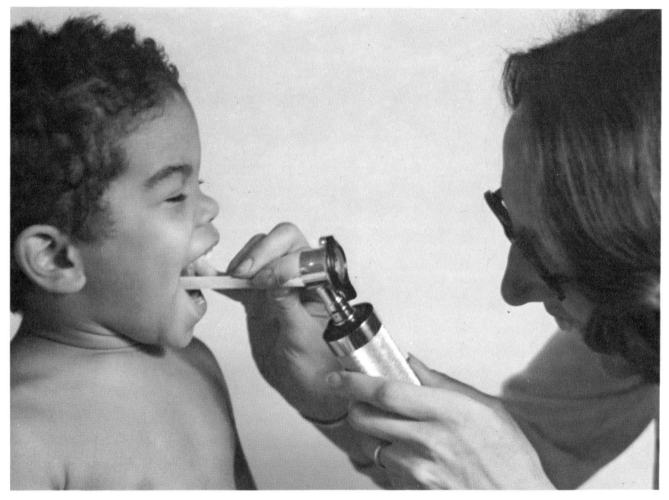

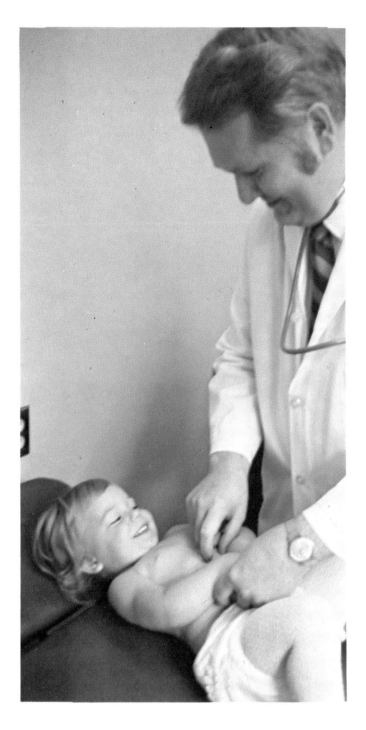

The doctor presses on your tummy, and sometimes that tickles a bit. The doctor looks in your ears with an otoscope,

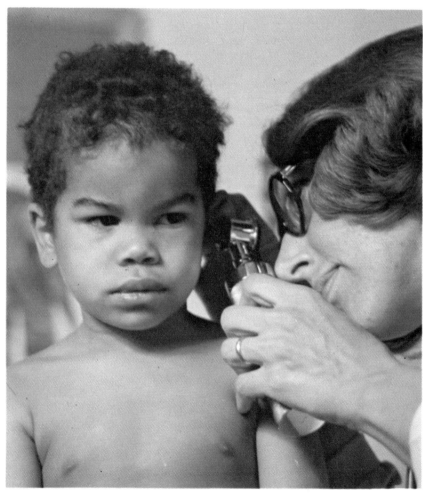

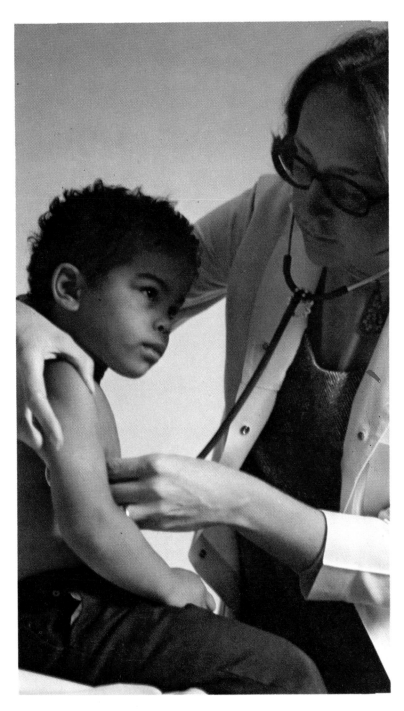

and listens to your heart and
your back and your stomach
with a stethoscope,

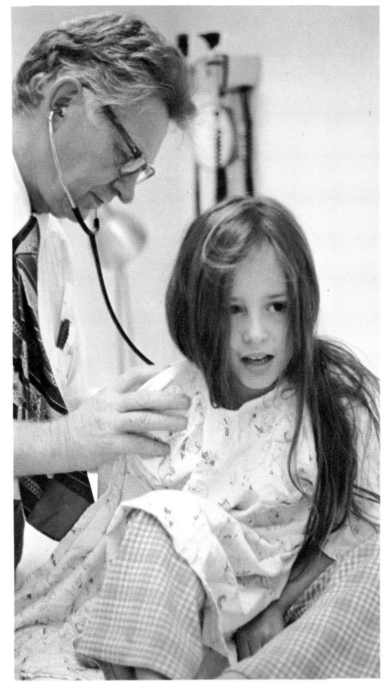

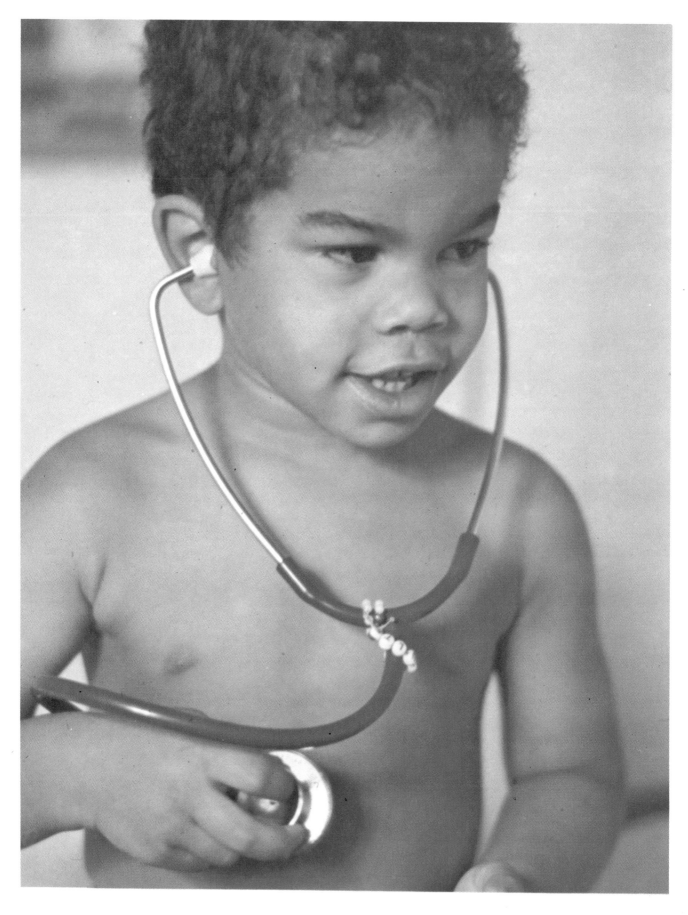

and may even let you use them on yourself.
That way you can see that the doctor can look
inside and listen inside certain parts of
your body. But nobody—not even a doctor—
can see or hear what you're thinking.

If the doctor gives you an injection—some people call it a "shot"—it might hurt for a little while. (It sometimes feels like a big pinch.) Doctors don't like to do anything to hurt people, but they know that injections protect people from getting sick and often make them better when they are sick. The hurt from the injection usually goes away very quickly.

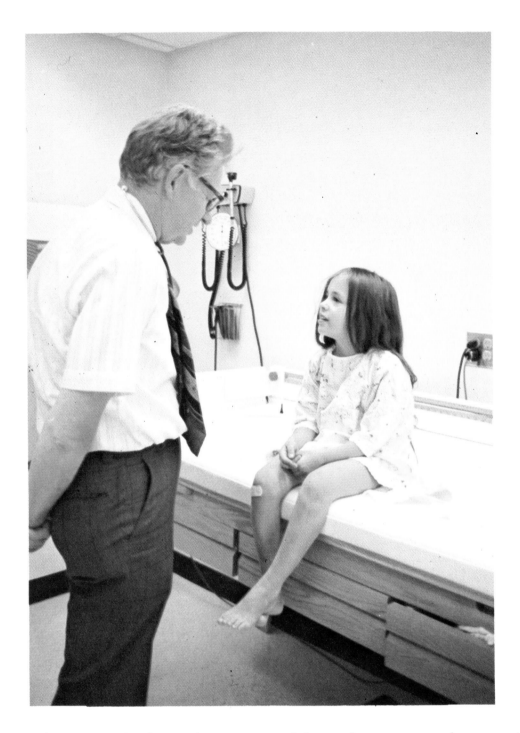

If you're wondering about anything that your doctor is doing to keep you well or make you feel better, just ask. Doctors can be honest about anything children wonder about.

After your time with the doctor is over,
then you go home.

You may want to play about being a doctor
yourself — doctor to your toys, doctor
to your friends.

Playing about something is one of the
best ways of knowing how you feel
about it.

• • •

GOING TO SCHOOL

Every year you see that bigger children get to go to school.

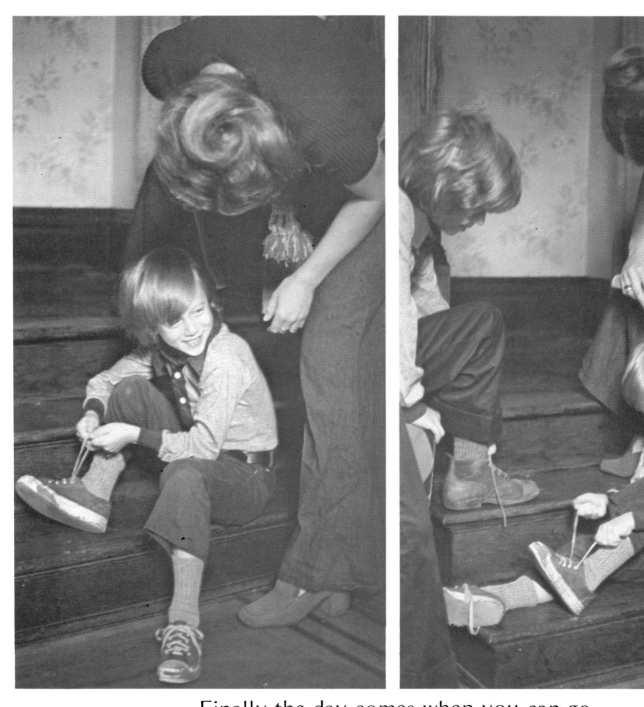

Finally the day comes when you can go.

Some people walk to school.
Some people ride in a car.
Some people ride in a bus.

Every school is different, but every
school has teachers and people who
come to learn.

There are different times to do things at school.
There's a time to get there.

There's a time to learn how to read.

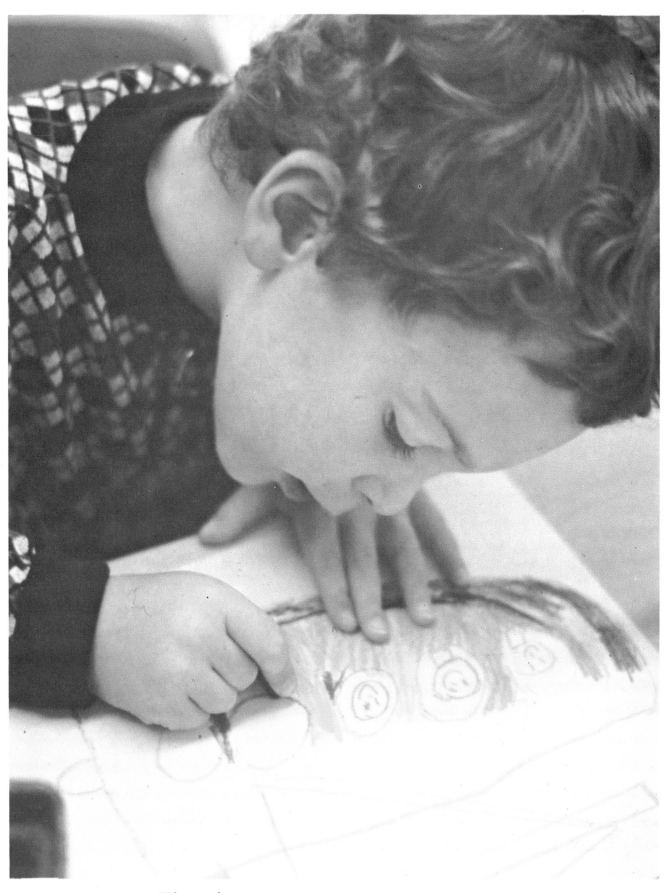

There's a time to color with crayons.

There's a time to play.

There's a time to wait for the teacher while the teacher helps another child.

In some schools, there's even a time to drink milk.

And in all schools, every day there's
a time to go home.

At first when you go to school there's lots to see that's new and different.

But sometimes you might wish for your parents or your grandparents while you're there. Your teachers can understand this because they were little once, too.

But teachers know that children really want to learn.
They help children understand "how much" and "how
many," how to read, and how to write their own words.

Teachers give children opportunities to make pictures and music, and explore.

They know that children want to do big things for themselves and that's why teachers are teachers. They want to help children learn.

Each day when you go home from school to
your own family, you have things you might want
to tell about school and the things you did there.

Grown-ups at home like to hear about what you're
learning in school so they can remember again what it
was like when they were little. Then they can tell you
how people keep on learning even when they don't go
to school anymore, and how the most important part
of school is learning *how* to learn and how to really *like*
to learn.

Going to school for children is like going to work for grown-ups. It's important. You can be proud when you feel you're ready to go.

• • •

GETTING A HAIRCUT

Sometimes young people as well as their mothers and fathers think that their hair would look better if it were shorter. That's why they get a haircut. (Hair and fingernails and toenails are the only things that grow on people that sometimes need to be trimmed and they are all things that don't hurt when they are cut.)

Some people have straight hair and other people
have curly hair. Some have dark hair and others have
light hair.

Some have short hair and some have long hair — but whatever kind *you* have is just the kind of hair that makes you look like YOU.

The people who cut hair are barbers and hairdressers.
That's their job and they know how to do it carefully.
Some mothers and fathers know how to cut hair well, too.
It may not be their job, but they care about their
children and so they do it carefully, too.

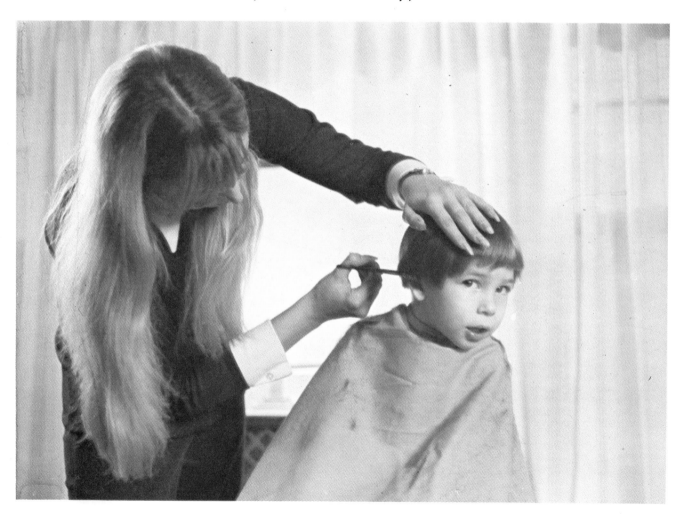

There are things about haircuts
that some children don't like.

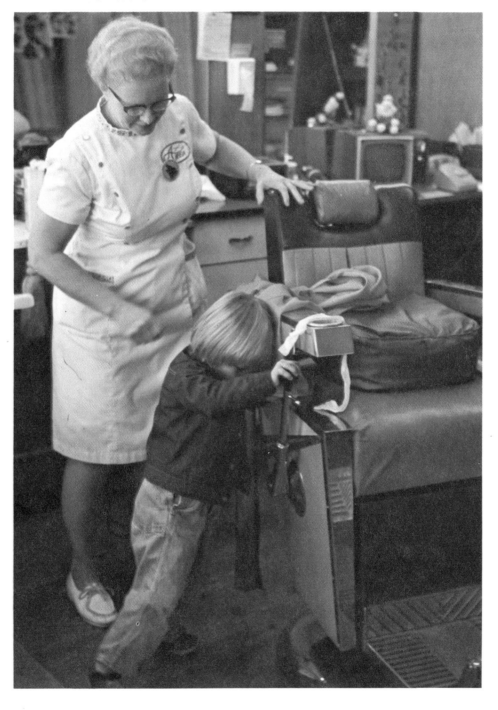

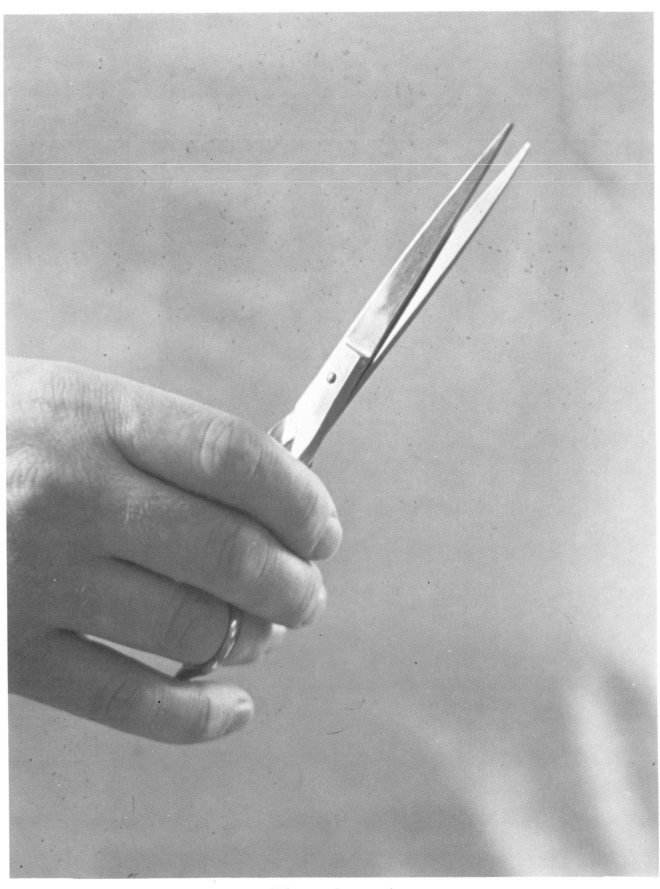

The scissors!

Sometimes when children look at the scissors
they wonder if the scissors might accidentally
cut something else besides their hair. Well,
the scissors are made to cut *only* hair — not ears
or noses or anything else — JUST HAIR.

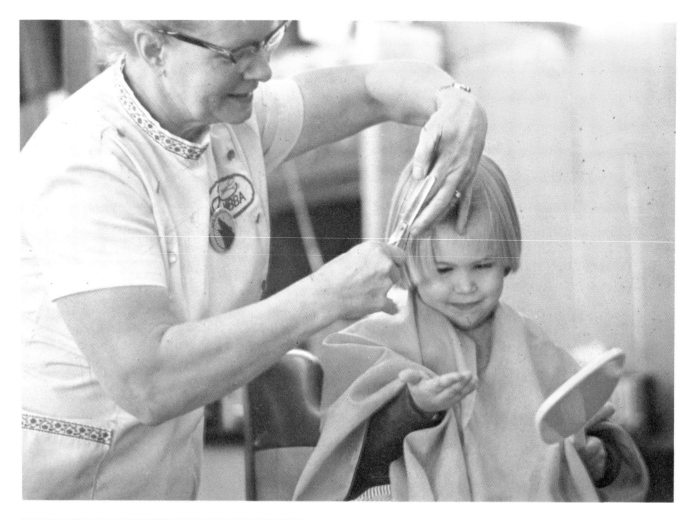

Many children don't like the way the little pieces of cut hair feel on their faces and necks. The person who cuts your hair usually brushes them away. You can use a handkerchief to brush them away, and if you miss a few you can wash them off when you take a bath.

There are some things about haircuts that
some children like a lot.

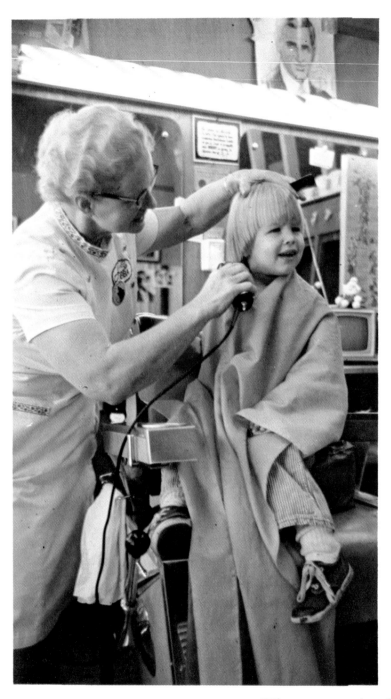

The sound of the clippers!

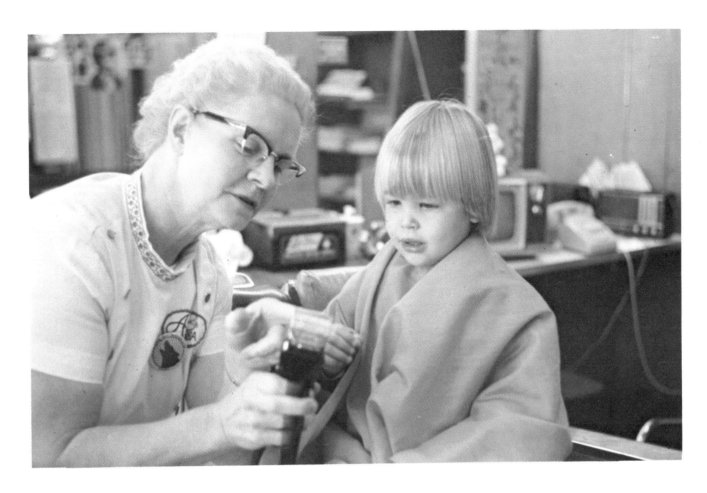

Sometimes the person who is cutting your
hair uses electric clippers and might let you
turn them on if you want.

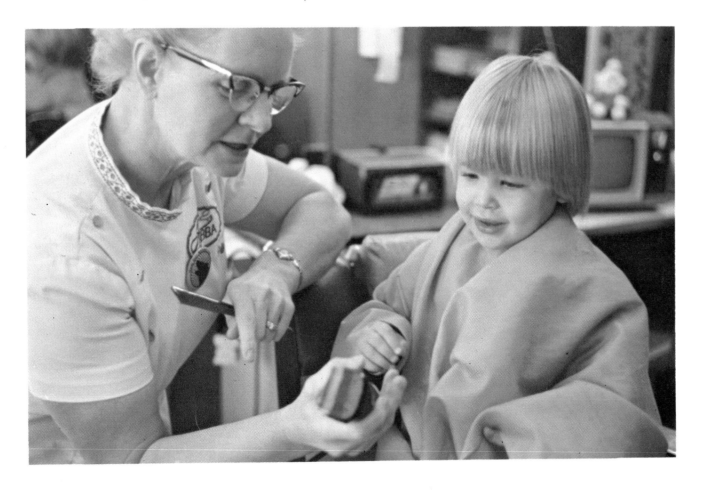

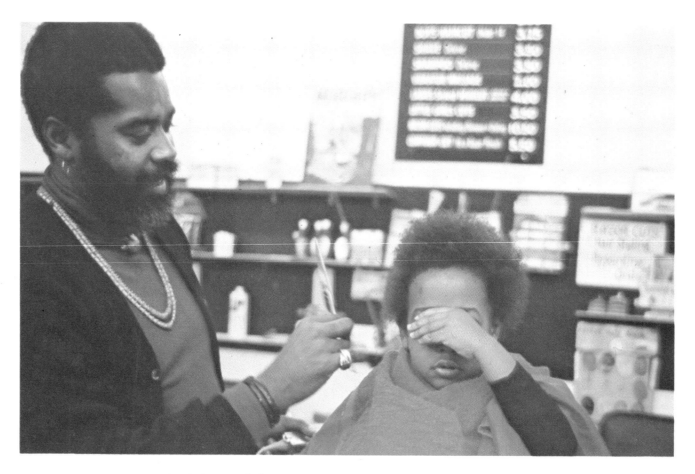

Some children like to tell by the sound and the feel whether the barber is using the clippers or the scissors.

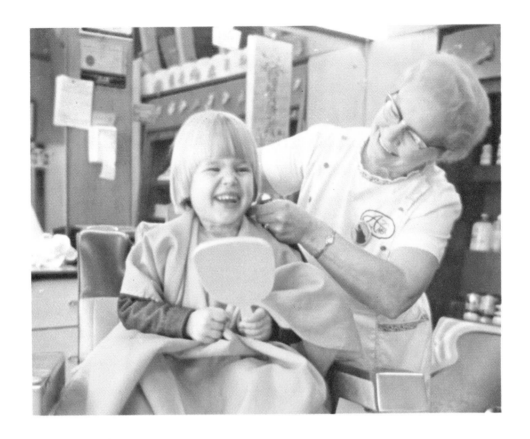

Sometimes it's hard to sit very quietly while you're getting a haircut, but that's the way you can help the person who's cutting your hair do the best job.

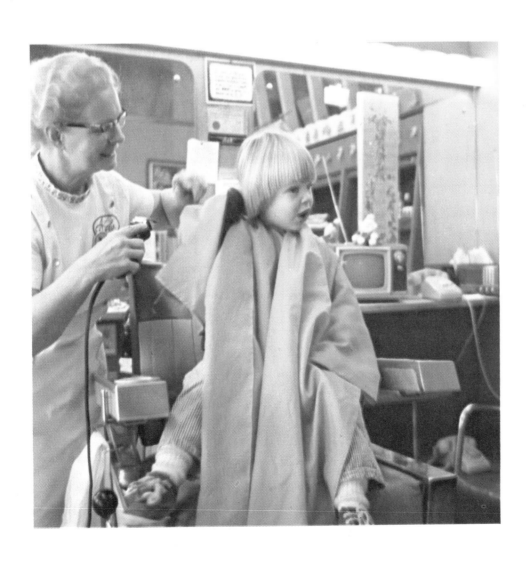

When your haircut is finished, your hair will be shorter. Then you can look in the mirror and see how you like it. If it's just exactly the way you want it, that's fine. If you are not sure that it is just exactly the way you want it, you *can* be sure that it will grow again.

THE END